REAL WORLD DATA

GRAPHING BUILDINGS AND STRUCTURES

Yvonne Thorpe

Heinemann
LIBRARY

Chicago, Illinois

© 2009 Heinemann Library
a division of Pearson Inc.
Chicago, Illinois

Customer Service 888–454–2279

Visit our website at www.heinemannraintree.com

Edited by Nancy Dickmann, Rachel Howells, and Sian Smith
Designed by Victoria Bevan and Geoff Ward
Illustrated by Geoff Ward
Picture Research by Mica Brancic

Originated by Modern Age
Printed and bound in China by Leo Paper Group

13 12 11 10 09
10 9 8 7 6 5 4 3 2 1

Library of Congress Cataloging-in-Publication Data
Thorpe, Yvonne.
  Graphing buildings and structures / Yvonne Thorpe.
    p. cm. -- (Real world data)
  Includes bibliographical references and index.
  ISBN 978-1-4329-1529-2 (hc) -- ISBN 978-1-4329-1544-5 (pb)
 1. Graphic methods. 2. Buildings. 3. Structural engineering. I. Title.
  QA90.T48 2008
  001.4'226--dc22
                                    2008018044

Acknowledgments
The publishers would like to thank the following for permission to reproduce photographs:
© Alamy, pp.**17** (David Noble Photography), **18** (Michele Falzone), **20** (Sue Cunningham Photographic), **22** (Asia, Tina Manley); © City of Melbourne p.**27**; © Corbis pp.**4** (John Harper), **6**, **8** (Construction Photography), **11** (Jose Fuste Raga), **13** (Star Ledger, Tony Kurdzuk), **14** (Underwood & Underwood), **16** (Bettmann), **24** (Hanan Isachar), **25** (Liba Taylor); © Getty Images pp.**10** (China Photos, Stringer), **12** (Time Life Pictures, Kaku Kurita), **19** (AFP).

Cover photograph of Watermark Tower, reproduced with permission of ©Corbis (Richard Cummins).

Every effort has been made to contact copyright holders of any material reproduced in this book. Any omissions will be rectified in subsequent printings if notice is given to the publishers.

The publishers would like to thank Harold Pratt for his assistance in the preparation of this book.

Disclaimer
All the Internet addresses (URLs) given in this book were valid at time of going to press. However, due to the dynamic nature of the Internet, some addresses may have changed, or sites may have changed or ceased to exist since publication. While the author and publishers regret any inconvenience this may cause readers, no responsibility for any such changes can be accepted by either the author or the publishers. It is recommended that adults supervise children on the Internet.

CONTENTS

Some words are printed in bold, **like this**. You can find out what they mean by looking in the glossary, on page 30.

STRUCTURES ALL AROUND

Buildings and structures are all around us. Our cities and towns are full of skyscrapers, office blocks, bridges, and tunnels, for example. Even in the countryside, you can almost always see a building somewhere: a house, a barn, or maybe a water tower.

Uses for structures

Most structures are built for practical uses. Bridges connect the land on each side of an obstacle, such as a river or road. Tunnels avoid obstacles, too, but by going under them instead of over them. Skyscrapers are built where big buildings have to fit in small spaces. If you cannot spread the building out sideways, building up into the air is the next best thing.

Giant sports stadiums are built so that tens of thousands of fans can watch their favorite teams compete.

Design

Not all structures are simply practical. Many are also built to look as attractive as possible. A new footbridge over the Thames River in London, England, for example, was designed to give great views of St. Paul's Cathedral. Skyscrapers such as the Chrysler Building in New York are built following the latest fashions. Taipei 101 in Taiwan has been designed to bring good luck to the people who work there.

 This is the Millennium Footbridge in London. Planning how many people will use a bridge helps **engineers** know how strong it needs to be.

Change through time

A graph turns numbers into a picture. Graphs often make **data** simpler and quicker to understand. This graph shows the increasing height of the world's tallest buildings, every 20 years for the last 100 years. The vertical axis (the line on the left) shows height. (1 meter equals 3.28 feet.) The horizontal axis (the line at the bottom) shows the year. You can see how the height of the buildings is rising as time goes by.

Date	Height of building	Name and location of building
1910	300 meters (984 feet)	Eiffel Tower, Paris, France
1930	319 meters (1,047 feet)	Chrysler Building, New York, USA
1950	381 meters (1,250 feet)	Empire State Building, New York, USA
1970	537 meters (1,762 feet)	Ostankino Tower, Moscow, Russia
1990	553 meters (1,814 feet)	CN Tower, Toronto, Canada
2010	800 meters* (2,625 feet)	Burj Dubai, United Arab Emirates

* This is the expected height for 2010. In 2008 the Burj Dubai reached 605 meters (1,985 feet) tall.

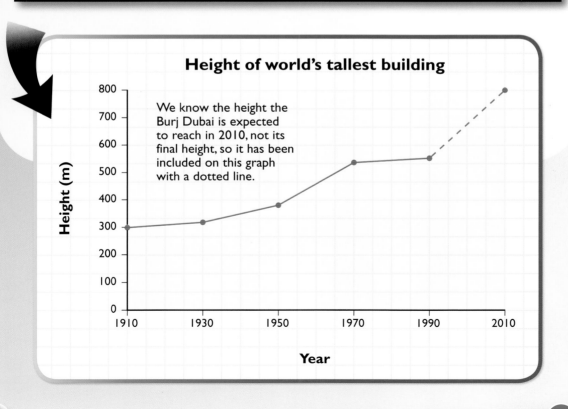

Height of world's tallest building

We know the height the Burj Dubai is expected to reach in 2010, not its final height, so it has been included on this graph with a dotted line.

Tunnels are probably the structures people find it easiest to forget about. After all, tunnels burrow along underground. You may have been through one in a car, but you usually only see the ends, where they pop out into the open air. Tunnels, however, do some very important jobs for us.

Toilet tunnels

Many people never think of it, but every time they use the toilet, they are at one end of a tunnel system. The toilet pipe eventually leads to tunnels called sewers, and they carry away our waste water. Many of the world's cities are now having trouble with their sewers. When the sewers were built over 100 years ago, they were big enough to take away all the waste. Today, though, lots more people live in the cities. The sewers have not grown at the same speed as the population and cannot cope with all the waste.

Tunnels for travel

Of course, not all tunnels are as disgusting inside as sewers. Tunnels are often used for transportation, especially in cities. Often building new roads and railroads on the city surface is too difficult, because there is no space for them. Instead, planners put the transportation system underground, in deep tunnels.

 Boston, Massachusetts, has a giant highway flowing under the city, as part of its Central Artery Tunnel Project.

WESTON HILLS TUNNEL

Line graphs

Line graphs can be used to show how things change over time. Here, you can see how the number of people living in towns and cities increased between 1950 and 2000. Charting population increase helps planners figure out whether more structures like homes, offices, sewers, and schools should be built.

The vertical axis (which runs up and down) on a graph is called the **y-axis**. The horizontal axis (which runs from side to side) is called the **x-axis**. The **scale** on each axis can be adjusted to make it possible to fit big amounts into a small space on the graph.

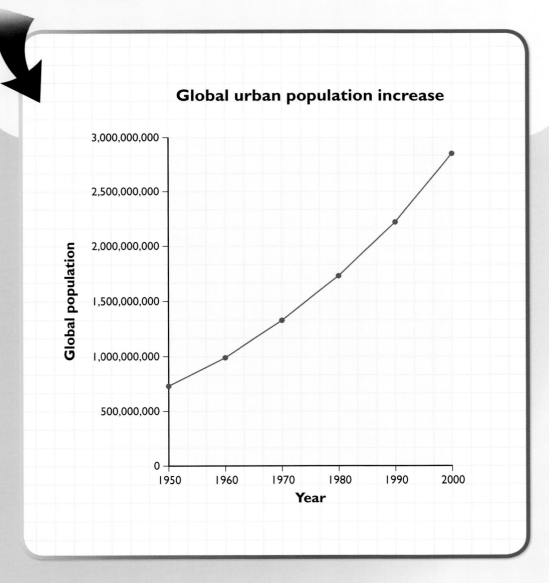

Global urban population increase

There are two main ways to build a large tunnel. Which one is used depends on how deep underground the tunnel will be and the type of soil in which it will be built.

Cut and cover tunnels

"Cut and cover tunnels" are often used when a shallow tunnel is going through soft soil. A deep trench is dug, the sides and roof are **reinforced**, and earth is piled back on top to make the tunnel.

Bored tunnels

Bored tunnels are hollowed out deep underground. Tunnel boring machines (TBMs) can eat their way through all kinds of soil and rock. As the TBM bores its way along, the tunnel is **shored up** to make sure it does not collapse.

 A tunnel boring machine waits to chew its way back underground.

Amazing tunnels

- The Channel Tunnel runs farther under the sea than any other tunnel. It travels below the waves of the English Channel between England and France for 39 kilometers (24 miles).
- The Lincoln Tunnel between New Jersey and New York is the world's busiest. It carries about 120,000 vehicles a day.

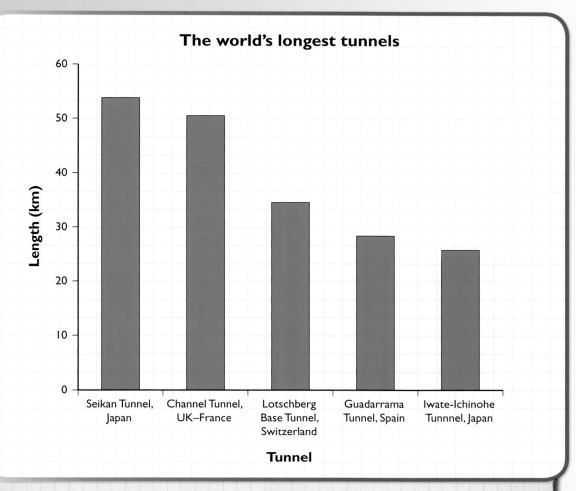

The world's longest tunnels

This bar chart allows you to see very quickly that the Seikan Tunnel in Japan is almost twice the length of the world's fifth-longest tunnel, which is also in Japan. (1 kilometer equals 0.62 mile.) It cannot show everything, though: you cannot see from the chart that the Channel Tunnel actually travels longer under the sea than the Seikan and is the world's longest undersea tunnel.

BRIDGES

Tunnels and bridges both do similar jobs. Like tunnels, bridges make it easier to get from one place to another, over obstacles such as roads or rivers. Bridges, though, have a big advantage over tunnels—they usually cost much less to build. Because of this, **engineers** usually only build tunnels if it would be impossible to build a bridge.

Bridge designs

The first bridge designs were very simple. They were probably something like a log dropped across a river, to let people cross without getting their feet wet. This design is known as a beam bridge.

Over time, bridges have become more and more complicated as they need to **span** bigger and bigger distances. These are some of the main types:

- Arch bridges were first used at the time of the Roman Empire (27 BCE to 476 CE). These were stronger than the simple bridges that had gone before, and could be used to cross wider rivers.
- Cantilever bridges are only supported at one end (like a drawbridge in a castle). Some cantilever bridges use two or more cantilevers, one from each side, to span a wide gap.
- In suspension bridges, the bridge hangs on strong cables from tall towers. Some of the world's biggest, most spectacular bridges are suspension bridges.

The Donghai Bridge in China is the world's longest sea-crossing bridge. It runs 32.5 kilometers (20 miles), joining the city of Shanghai to the port of Yangshan.

The Valentré Bridge in Cahors, France, is an arch bridge. Its towers were built to defend the bridge against attackers.

Bar charts

Bar charts can be either horizontal or vertical, yet both types show the same information. Sometimes it makes more sense to show the information horizontally. The bar chart below shows the length of the world's eight longest bridges. (1 kilometer equals 0.62 mile.) It is a horizontal bar graph, which is useful when showing this sort of information about length.

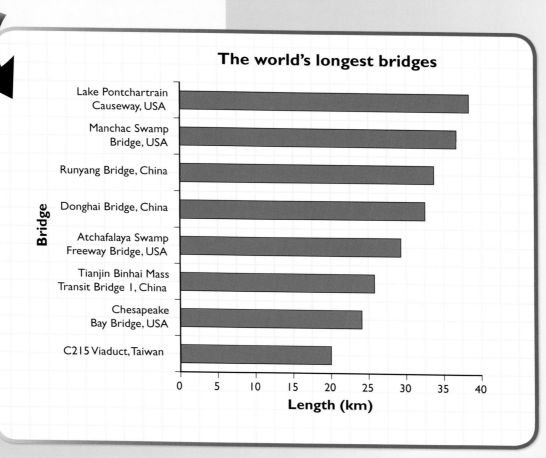

The world's longest bridges

Bridge / Length (km):
- Lake Pontchartrain Causeway, USA
- Manchac Swamp Bridge, USA
- Runyang Bridge, China
- Donghai Bridge, China
- Atchafalaya Swamp Freeway Bridge, USA
- Tianjin Binhai Mass Transit Bridge 1, China
- Chesapeake Bay Bridge, USA
- C215 Viaduct, Taiwan

THE WORLD'S BUSIEST BRIDGES

The world's busiest bridges are large suspension bridges. These bridges often cross wide bodies of water, allowing travelers to avoid long journeys around the water. As a result, they carry ever-increasing numbers of people traveling in cars, buses, and trains.

One of the world's busiest suspension bridges is the George Washington Bridge between New Jersey and Manhattan, in New York City. The bridge opened to traffic in 1931, with six **lanes** of traffic. As the number of cars has grown, the bridge has had to add more and more lanes to cope with the traffic. In 1946 two more lanes were added, making eight in total. Then, in 1962 a whole new **deck** running below the first was opened, with another six lanes for vehicles to use. Today, roughly 300,000 vehicles cross the George Washington Bridge every day.

 The Akashi-Kaikyo Bridge has the longest **span** of any suspension bridge, at 1,991 meters (6,532 feet). The bridge crosses the Akashi Strait between the city of Kobe and Awasji Island in Japan.

 When it was built, the George Washington Bridge had the biggest single span of any bridge in the world.

Journey planning

Pictograms use pictures to represent **data** in a graph. This pictogram of traffic flowing across the George Washington Bridge would be useful to anyone planning a journey. One car shape stands for 1,000 cars. The different colors show how much of the traffic goes in each direction. Crossing west-to-east is in red, and east-to-west is in yellow. You can see that between 3:00 p.m. and 4:00 p.m., it is much better to be traveling eastward than westward!

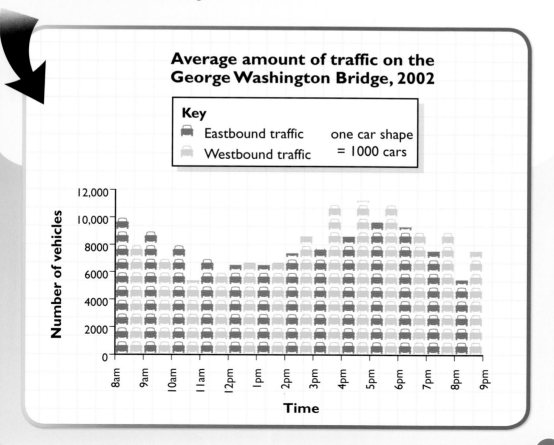

Average amount of traffic on the George Washington Bridge, 2002

Key
🚗 Eastbound traffic   one car shape
🚗 Westbound traffic   = 1000 cars

Number of vehicles (y-axis: 0, 2000, 4000, 6000, 8000, 10,000, 12,000)

Time (x-axis: 8am, 9am, 10am, 11am, 12pm, 1pm, 2pm, 3pm, 4pm, 5pm, 6pm, 7pm, 8pm, 9pm)

The world's giant suspension bridges are pretty spectacular—but if there is one type of building that can outdo them, it is skyscrapers! These giant buildings tower over every other structure on Earth.

The first skyscrapers

Hundreds of years ago, "skyscraper" was the word used to describe the tallest masts of the biggest sailing ships. Then, in the 1800s, buildings with many **stories** started to be built in New York City and, especially, Chicago. No one had ever seen such tall buildings before, and people started calling them "skyscrapers."

Skyscraper technology

The first skyscrapers could be built because the **technology** of structures had changed. **Architects** were able to plan buildings that used a steel framework to support the buildings they designed. This framework was much stronger than bricks piled one on top of the other, which had been the old way of building tall structures. The steel framework could support the extra weight of a taller building.

Every time new technology has been developed, architects have been able to build taller skyscrapers. As they have been able to use stronger steel and concrete, the maximum height of buildings has increased. The architects of the late 1800s would not recognize the skyscraper technology of today!

 Many people think the Home Insurance Building in Chicago was the world's first skyscraper. It was built in 1885 and demolished in 1931.

Double bar charts

Bar charts can tell two different stories at the same time. The table below shows the world's tallest buildings through time, ranked by their highest point. (1 meter equals 3.28 feet.) But giant antennae are sometimes added to tall buildings. When these are included, the ranking becomes confusing. In the two-column bar chart below, it is much easier to understand. The **key** tells you what each color means.

Building	Year	Highest point of building	Height to tip, including radio masts, antennae, etc.
Chrysler Building, USA	1930	282 meters	319 meters
Empire State Building, USA	1931	381 meters	449 meters
World Trade Center, USA	1972	417 meters	528 meters
Sears Tower, USA	1974	442 meters	527 meters
Petronas Towers, Malaysia	1998	403 meters	452 meters
Taipei 101, Taiwan	2003	448 meters	509 meters

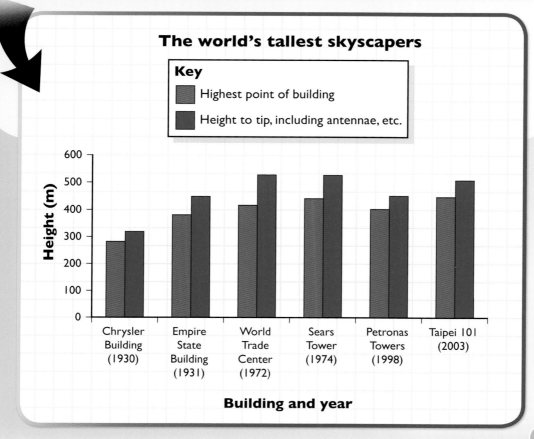

The world's tallest skyscapers

Key
- Highest point of building
- Height to tip, including antennae, etc.

If you stop people in the street and ask them to name the world's most famous skyscraper, there is a good chance many of them will say, "The Empire State Building"! The Empire State Building is in New York City. What is it that made this skyscraper so well known?

Battle for the top spot

Between 1873 and 1931, there were 11 holders of the record for World's Tallest Building. Nine of the eleven had been in New York. The city was the hot spot in the battle for the "World's Tallest" title! The title changed hands twice in 1930 alone, and in 1931 the Empire State Building took over from the nearby Chrysler Building as the world's tallest building. Incredibly, it would then hold the title for the next 40 years. After that time, the building had appeared in so many movies, stories, and radio shows that it was famous around the world.

 The Empire State Building is shown here under construction in the 1930s. This was a "Golden Age" of skyscrapers, when many of the world's most famous skyscrapers were built.

Empire State facts
- Mohawk Indians were among the workers on the Empire State Building, and they became famous for their high-level skills.
- The mast at the top was originally meant as an airship landing base.
- In 1945 elevator operator Betty Lou Oliver survived when her elevator plunged 75 floors. This is still the world record for the longest elevator drop ever survived.

The Chrysler Building (front) is shown here with the Empire State Building in the background. These two skyscrapers are the most famous examples of an architectural style called **Art Deco**.

Pie charts

Pie charts are a good way of showing percentages of a whole. They show how different parts make up a whole picture. This pie chart shows how the votes were divided when people in the United States voted for their favorite buildings. The Empire State Building came first, with 18 percent of the votes.

Survey of the United States' favorite buildings

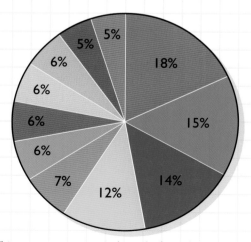

This survey was carried out before the terrorist attacks on the World Trade Center in 2001.

Key

- Empire State Building
- Other buildings
- World Trade Center
- Chrysler Building
- St. Patrick's Cathedral
- Golden Gate Bridge
- White House
- Falling Water
- Lincoln Memorial
- U.S. Capitol
- Bellagio Hotel

The Empire State lost the title of World's Tallest Building in 1972. Since then, several other skyscrapers have held the record. In 2003 Taipei 101, in Taipei City, Taiwan, officially became the world's tallest building.

Taipei 101 is an amazing 509 meters (1,670 feet) tall. If it is hard to imagine just how big that is, think of it like this. If 145 large elephants somehow managed to stand on each other's heads, only the 145th elephant would be able to see over Taipei 101.

Lucky eight

In Taiwan, the number eight is thought to be lucky. Because of this, Taipei 101 has eight levels. Each level has eight **stories**. The skyscraper also has four circles at the base, to represent coins. These are supposed to make sure that any businesses inside the building are successful.

 Taipei 101, in Taiwan, became the world's tallest building in 2003.

The new tallest building?

In 2009 a new building is likely to overtake Taipei 101 as the world's official tallest building. This is the Burj Dubai skyscraper, in Dubai. The final height is being kept secret until the building opens, but rumors say that Burj Dubai will be over 800 meters (2,625 feet) tall—perhaps even higher.

 The Burj Dubai was under construction in 2008.

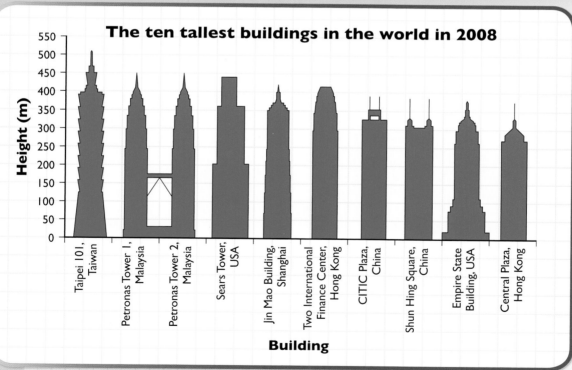

The ten tallest buildings in the world in 2008

Height (m): 0, 50, 100, 150, 200, 250, 300, 350, 400, 450, 500, 550

Buildings:
- Taipei 101, Taiwan
- Petronas Tower 1, Malaysia
- Petronas Tower 2, Malaysia
- Sears Tower, USA
- Jin Mao Building, Shanghai
- Two International Finance Center, Hong Kong
- CITIC Plaza, China
- Shun Hing Square, China
- Empire State Building, USA
- Central Plaza, Hong Kong

Building

 This pictogram shows the world's tallest buildings in 2008, before the official opening of the Burj Dubai. (1 meter equals 3.28 feet.) The Petronas Towers are counted as two buildings.

DAMS

A dam is a barrier across a river that slows or stops the water from flowing. Dams come in lots of shapes and sizes. The biggest dams are among the largest structures on Earth.

Early dams

The first dams were built of wood, rock, and earth. They were used to create lakes of water, which were used as a water store during dry weather or for watering food crops. These simple structures could only be used to dam small rivers.

Later, the **engineers** of the Roman Empire (27 BCE to 476 CE) began to build dams made of specially cut stone. These were stronger than any dams that had been built before. In fact, some are still in use today.

The Itaipu Dam, on the border between Brazil and Paraguay, produces electricity for the surrounding area.

Technology and dams

As building **technology** improved, people began to make stronger and stronger dams. Soon they could hold back huge amounts of water. Dams built in the United States in the late 1800s and early 1900s, such as the Hoover Dam, created giant **reservoirs**. The dams made it possible to **irrigate** dry regions in the west of the country so they could be settled.

Modern dams

Today, dams do two main jobs. They still create huge stores of water for farms, businesses, and people. Dams also provide **hydroelectric** power. Once enough water has built up behind the dam, some is released. It shoots through small gaps, at very high speed. The rushing water is used to create electricity.

Energy pie

This simple pie chart shows the different sources of the world's electricity. Almost all comes from burning **fossil fuels**—oil, coal, and gas. These release **greenhouse gases**, which are harming Earth's environment. Only a tiny slice of the **energy** pie comes from hydroelectric power, which does not release fossil fuels.

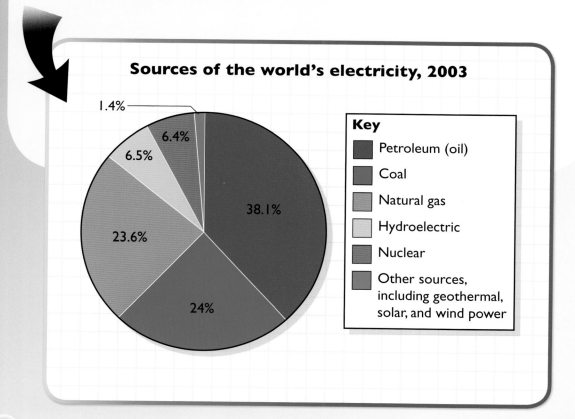

Sources of the world's electricity, 2003

1.4%
6.4%
6.5%
38.1%
23.6%
24%

Key
- Petroleum (oil)
- Coal
- Natural gas
- Hydroelectric
- Nuclear
- Other sources, including geothermal, solar, and wind power

THE THREE GORGES DAM

The Three Gorges Dam in China is the world's largest. It is the biggest engineering project in China since the building of the Great Wall, which runs for about 7,300 kilometers (4,500 miles) in total. Like the Great Wall, the Three Gorges Dam is visible from space. It is the largest structure ever made of concrete.

The Three Gorges Dam is almost 200 meters (660 feet) high and over 2 kilometers (1.2 miles) wide. The **reservoir** behind the dam is 660 kilometers (410 miles) long, and holds as much water as Lake Superior in North America. The dam flooded a vast area of land. Whole villages were swallowed by the rising water levels and have now disappeared under water. Over one million people had to be moved from their homes as a result.

Hydroelectric powerhouse

The Three Gorges Dam was built to provide power for China's growing cities and industries. The dam's 26 **hydroelectric** turbines convert the **energy** of flowing water into electricity. Six more turbines will be added by 2010. Then, the dam will be able to produce almost twice as much power as the next most powerful dam, the Itaipu Dam in South America.

 This photograph shows part of China's giant Three Gorges Dam.

Problems comparing big with small

The table below shows the world's largest dams. The **volume** of the dam tells us how much water the dam holds. (1 cubic meter equals 35.3 cubic feet.) Using a bar chart to show this information makes it much easier to compare the sizes of the different dams. It is difficult to show all the information from the table, however, because the Three Gorges Dam is so much larger than the rest of the world's largest dams. If the Three Gorges Dam were included on the bar chart below, its bar would be 275 centimeters (108 inches) high and stretch off the page!

Dam name	Country	Volume of dam, m³
Three Gorges	China	39,300,000
Syncrude Tailings	Canada	540,000
Chapetón	Argentina	296,200
Pati	Argentina	238,180
New Cornelia Tailings	USA	209,500
Tarbela	Pakistan	121,720
Kambaratinsk	Kyrgyzstan	112,200

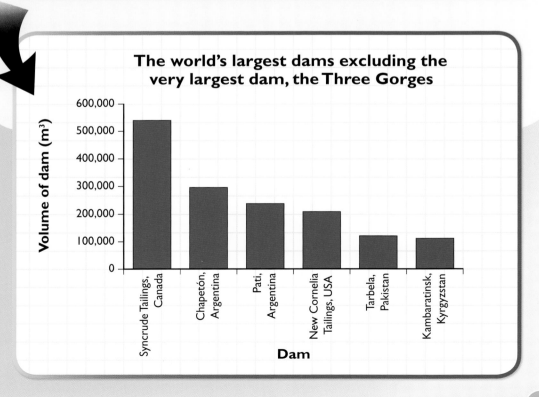

The world's largest dams excluding the very largest dam, the Three Gorges

DOMES

What links the oldest **Islamic shrine** on Earth and the Atlanta Falcons football team? Both take shelter underneath domes! The Dome of the Rock in Jerusalem, Israel, is the oldest Islamic shrine; the Falcons play at the Georgia Dome. Domes are among Earth's most amazing structures.

What is a dome?

A dome is a roof in the shape of half of a round ball. Its shape is like a giant-sized tennis ball cut in half. Not all domes look perfectly like a half circle when seen from the side. Some domes look like the half tennis ball crushed from above, so they are flatter than usual. These are sometimes called saucer domes. Other domes look more as though the tennis ball had been crushed in from the sides. These are taller than usual and are sometimes called onion domes, because they look a bit like an onion.

 This is the Dome of the Rock in Jerusalem. The dome was gold-plated during the twentieth century by the Grand Mufti of Jerusalem, its Muslim ruler from 1921 to 1948.

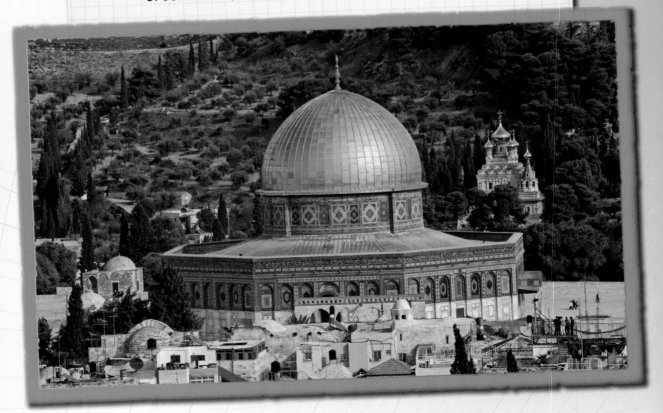

Building a dome

Domes were traditionally built as a series of arches. Each arch passes through the same point at the top of the dome, but starts and finishes at a different point on the base. Some domes are made of solid stone, so the arches touch each other and look like a flat surface. In other domes the arches are visible, like a skeleton supporting the skin of the roof.

 The world's widest dome is the Millennium Dome in London.

Dome-tastic!

In 1998 a new dome became the world's largest. The Millennium Dome in London, England, is 365 meters (1,198 feet) across. This bar chart shows how record-sized domes have gotten bigger through time. (1 meter equals 3.28 feet.)

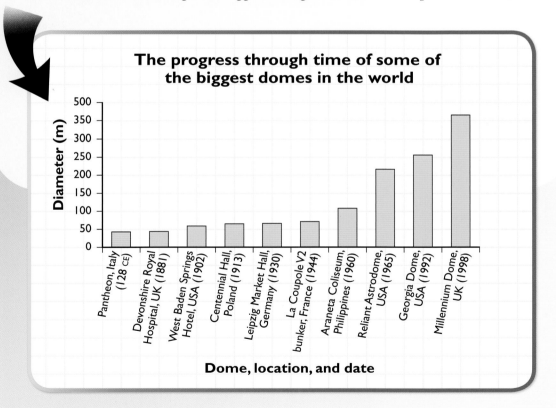

The progress through time of some of the biggest domes in the world

Most office buildings use up a lot of **energy**. This energy is usually made by burning **fossil fuels**, which releases **greenhouse gases**. These cause **global warming**, the slow increase in Earth's average temperature. Global warming is responsible for melting the polar ice caps, which causes an increase in sea level, and for disastrous changes in our weather and climate.

Building emissions

This pie chart shows where our greenhouse gas emissions come from. Building structures creates 8 percent of the greenhouse gases released each year—but that is not the end of the story. Once built, the structures use most of the electricity made in power stations, which release large amounts of greenhouse gases. Overall, building and maintaining structures causes about one-third of our greenhouse gas emissions.

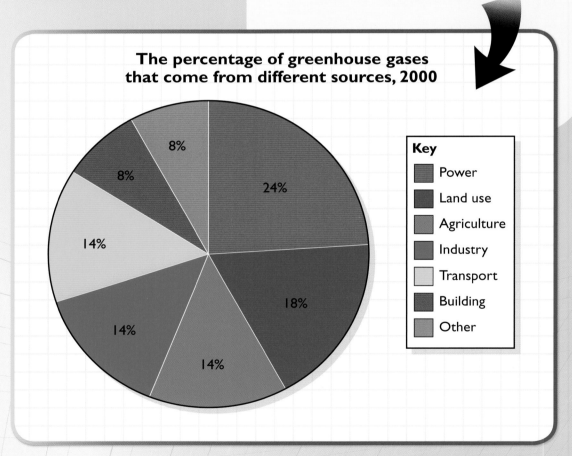

The percentage of greenhouse gases that come from different sources, 2000

24%
18%
14%
14%
14%
8%
8%

Key
- Power
- Land use
- Agriculture
- Industry
- Transport
- Building
- Other

CH₂, Australia

CH$_2$ is short for "Council House 2." It is a local government office building in Melbourne, Australia. CH$_2$ claims to be the world's most environmentally friendly office building.

Energy saving

To make sure it has as little effect on the environment as possible, CH$_2$ is filled with energy-saving features:

- The north side is shielded from the sun's heat by a "vertical garden" of vines. This keeps the building cool in the hot Australian sunshine and means air conditioning is not needed.

- Inside, CH$_2$ is heated or cooled using the sun's energy, water, and **wind turbines**. For cooling, cool air is dragged into the top of the building and circulated through each floor.

- Sixty percent of the building's hot water comes from **solar panels** on the roof.

Eco homes

Today, many homes are being built with eco features similar to CH$_2$'s. Solar panels, wind turbines, and the use of natural materials for **insulation** are becoming increasingly common.

wind turbine

 The CH$_2$ building in Melbourne, Australia, opened in August 2006.

CHART SMARTS

Data is information about our world. It can be words, such as a list of skyscrapers. Data can be numbers, such as the number of cars that cross a bridge each day. It can be contained in pictures—for example, photographs of a valley before and after it has been flooded by a dam. Graphs can make all kinds of data easier to understand.

Pie charts

A pie chart is used to show the different parts of a whole picture. A pie chart is the best way to show how something is divided up. These charts show information as different sized portions of a circle. They can help you compare proportions. You can easily see which section is the largest slice of the "pie."

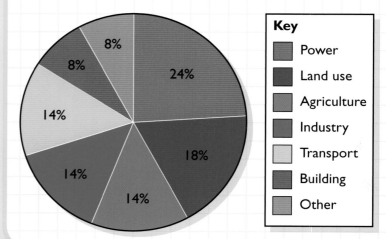

The percentage of greenhouse gases that come from different sources, 2000

24%
8%
8%
14%
18%
14%
14%

Key
- Power
- Land use
- Agriculture
- Industry
- Transport
- Building
- Other

Bar charts

Bar charts are a good way to compare amounts of different things. Bar charts have a vertical **y-axis** showing the **scale**, and a horizontal **x-axis** showing the different types of information. They can show one or more different types of bars.

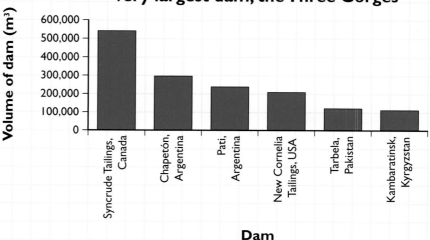

The world's largest dams excluding the very largest dam, the Three Gorges

Volume of dam (m³)

600,000
500,000
400,000
300,000
200,000
100,000
0

Syncrude Tailings, Canada · Chapetón, Argentina · Pati, Argentina · New Cornelia Tailings, USA · Tarbela, Pakistan · Kambaratinsk, Kyrgyzstan

Dam

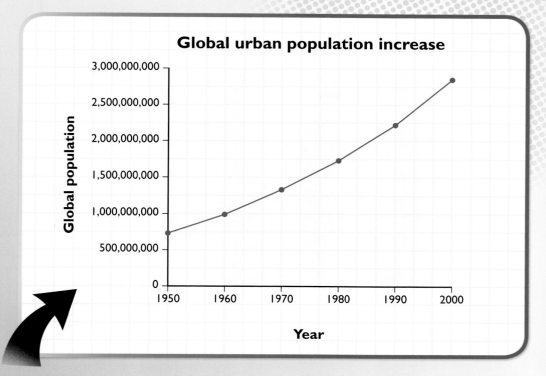

Global urban population increase

Line graphs

Line graphs use lines to connect points on a graph. They can be used to show how something changes over time. Time, such as months, is usually shown on the x-axis.

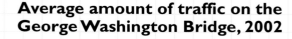

Pictograms

A pictogram uses pictures to show data. Each picture can stand for one unit or more than one unit. A **key** tells you how to interpret the graph.

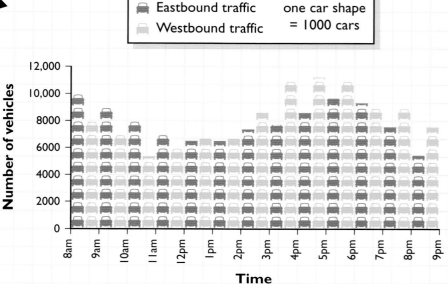

Average amount of traffic on the George Washington Bridge, 2002

Key		
🚗 Eastbound traffic	one car shape	
🚗 Westbound traffic	= 1000 cars	

GLOSSARY

architect person whose job is to design buildings

Art Deco style of architecture and design that was most popular in the 1930s. Art Deco used combinations of straight lines and simple shapes such as circles and arcs.

data information, often in the form of numbers

deck on bridges and other structures that are open to the outside, a deck is a level. Roads and railroads cross bridges on a deck, for example.

energy ability to do work—for example, powering a car or a light

engineer person who uses science in designing buildings, structures, and complicated devices such as engines

fossil fuel coal, oil, or natural gas. These are all fuels that are found in the ground and have taken millions of years to form.

global warming slow rise in Earth's temperature, which most scientists agree is caused by human actions (mainly burning fossil fuels)

greenhouse gas gas that holds heat inside Earth's atmosphere. Greenhouse gases are released when fossil fuels are burned.

hydroelectric describing electricity produced using the energy of flowing water

insulation material that can keep an object from changing how hot or cold it is

irrigate supply land or crops with water

Islamic shrine place where followers of the Islam religion go to worship because it is associated with an especially holy person

key explanation of the colors and symbols used on a diagram

lane division of a road, along which vehicles can travel

reinforce strengthen

reservoir large store of water, usually stored for human use—to drink, water crops, or use in industry

scale relationship between the marks on a graph's axis and the measurement the graph is showing. (For example, one mark on the y-axis might represent 1,000 miles.)

shore up support

solar panel flat panel that gathers the sun's energy and uses it to heat water or produce electricity

span gap between two points. In bridges, a span is the stretch between two places where the bridge touches its supports.

story level of a building, also known as a floor

technology use of science for practical purposes, such as creating new building techniques or building new machines

volume amount of space taken up by an object

wind turbine propeller-like device mounted on a tower or mast, which creates electricity from the power of the wind

x-axis horizontal line on a graph

y-axis vertical line on a graph

FURTHER INFORMATION

Books

Briscoe, Diana. *Bridge Building: Bridge Designs and How They Work.* Bloomington, Minn.: Red Brick Learning, 2004.

Goodman, Susan E. *Skyscraper.* New York: Alfred A. Knopf, 2004.

Hile, Kevin. *Dams and Levees.* Detroit: Kidhaven, 2007.

Oxlade, Chris. *Building Amazing Structures: Dams.* Chicago: Heinemann Library, 2006.

Oxlade, Chris. *Skyscraper: Uncovering Technology.* Richmond Hill, Ont.: Firefly, 2006.

Websites

The "archkidecture" website is packed with information on interesting structures and what they are made from. Find out about projects you can try yourself.
www.archkidecture.org

This website has information on the Empire State Building. Click on "Virtual tour" to see photos of the building and for spectacular views of New York City from the top.
www.esbnyc.org/kids/index.cfm

Find out about the different kinds of bridge, when they first became popular, and how they are used today. Watch a video about drawbridges.
www.howstuffworks.com/bridge.htm

This is the home page for Council House 2 in Melbourne, Australia, which is one of the world's most environmentally friendly office buildings. Look at photos of Council House 2 as it was being built and find out how the building works.
www.melbourne.vic.gov.au/info.cfm?top=171&pg=1933

INDEX